Bringing the Gospel to Covenant Children

FAMILY GUIDANCE SERIES

By Joel R. Beeke

The church must maintain the divinely ordered role of the family to establish a godly heritage. In this ongoing series, Dr. Joel R. Beeke offers pastoral insight and biblical direction for building strong Christian families.

Books in the series:
Bringing the Gospel to Covenant Children
Family Worship
The Family at Church

Bringing the Gospel to Covenant Children

Joel R. Beeke

REFORMATION HERITAGE BOOKS
Grand Rapids, Michigan

Bringing the Gospel to Covenant Children
© 2001, 2010 by Joel R. Beeke

Reformation Heritage Books
3070 29th St. SE
Grand Rapids, MI 49512
616-977-0889
e-mail: orders@heritagebooks.org
website: www.heritagebooks.org

Printed in the United States of America
21 22 23 24 25 26 / 10 9 8 7 6 5 4 3

Library of Congress Cataloging-in-Publication Data

Beeke, Joel R., 1952-
  Bringing the gospel to covenant children / Joel R. Beeke.
      p. cm. — (Family guidance series)
  Includes bibliographical references and index.
   ISBN 978-1-60178-117-8 (paperack : alk. paper) 1. Christian
education—Home training. 2. Christian education of children.
I. Title.
  BV1590.B44 2010
  248.8'45—dc22
                              2010047162

---

*For additional Reformed literature, both new and used,
request a free book list from the above address.*

With gratitude for

Steve Renkema and **Jay Collier**

great God-fearing friends, brothers in Christ,
and conscientious fathers,
who love sound Reformed books
almost as much as I do!

Thanks so much for all your hard work
as RHB's manager and director of publishing.
You are appreciated far more than you know.

Contents

Understanding the Need 1

Church growth books and manuals flood the market. Surprisingly few address internal growth through the Holy Spirit sovereignly blessing the raising of children in covenantal truth. Yet, historically, Reformed Christians have acknowledged that their most solid, genuine church growth has been through the conversion of youth reared in the church. Charles Spurgeon wrote to Edward Payson Hammond, author of *The Conversion of Children*, "My conviction is that our converts from among children are among the very best we have. I should judge them to have been more numerously genuine than any other class, more constant, and in the long run more solid."[1]

Andrew Bonar concurred. He also wrote to Hammond, saying, "In awakenings that have been given us, the cases of young people have been as entirely satisfactory as any cases we have had. If conversion be God's work, in which the Holy Spirit reveals Christ to

---

1. London: Morgan and Scott, n.d., 153.

the soul, surely His work can take place in children as really as in the old."[2]

Children raised in the church need to hear the gospel, that is, the evangel, every bit as much as adults. They too need to be born again. They too need to be evangelized in dependency on the Holy Spirit. In this book we will focus on three concerns:

1. The need for evangelizing covenant children,
2. The content of such evangelizing, and
3. The means for such evangelizing.

Understanding the Need

First, let me define the terms: By "covenant children" I mean those children born to at least one confessing parent (1 Cor. 7:14), who are baptized, and are growing up in the community of the church, with all the riches and privileges that entails, such as being placed under the prayers of the church and the preaching, invitations, and warnings of God's Word.[3] By "evangelize" or "evangelizing" I mean presenting the gospel of Christ the Savior as the one thing needful in the lives of desperate sinners, including our covenant children, praying that by Spirit-worked faith and repentance they may be drawn to God through Christ, grow in Him, and

---

2. Ibid., 158.

3. Susan Hunt, *Heirs of the Covenant: Leaving a Legacy of Faith for the Next Generation* (Wheaton, Ill.: Crossway Books, 1998), 98–102; Kay Arthur, *Our Covenant God* (Colorado Springs: Waterbrook Press, 1999).

serve Him as Lord in the fellowship of His church and in the extension of His kingdom in the world.

Today, many parents who have confessed their faith and whose children have been baptized are not adequately evangelizing, i.e., bringing the gospel to, their covenant children. Reasons for this include the following:

- Some parents confuse their children by living inconsistent and impure lives. They have faulty views of their covenant responsibilities toward their children, which leads them to respond inappropriately to the spiritual concerns and questions of their children. They often misrepresent God, election, sin, and the gospel to their children.

- Some parents abuse their children by prompting premature professions of faith through the altar call system or through "easy believism." They offer verbal assurance of salvation to their children without seeing biblical fruits of salvation. Or else, they err to the other extreme by treating their children like adults in this matter, expecting too much from them.[4]

- Some parents neglect their children by ignoring their spiritual needs, by not stressing the importance of the scriptural doctrines of grace, and by

4. Charles Spurgeon, *"Come, Ye Children": A Book for Parents and Teachers on the Christian Training of Children* (Pasadena, Tex.: Pilgrim Publications, n.d.), 14.

underestimating the challenge of our wicked and tempting times.[5]

- Some parents fail their children because they do not believe that God can convert them. They do not realize that more Christians have been converted in their youth than during any other stage of life. Such failures caused Robert Murray M'Cheyne to say in the 1850s, "Jesus has reason to complain of us, that He can do no mighty work in our Sabbath-schools, because of our unbelief. Let us pray for the children. Let us labour for the children. Let us hope for the children."[6]

A biblical view of our covenant children would greatly enhance our attempts to evangelize them properly. Before explaining that, let us first examine two errors that many evangelical parents make today in viewing their covenant children:

1. They *overestimate* the covenant relationship. Specifically, some parents overestimate the significance of their children's baptismal membership in the visible church. They view the covenant as a replacement for the regeneration and conversion of their children. This is particularly true of those who adhere to Abraham

---

5. Timothy Sisemore, *Of Such is the Kingdom: Nurturing Children in the Light of Scripture* (Fearn, Ross-shire: Christian Focus, 2000), 9–22.

6. Hammond, 163.

Kuyper's view of covenant children called "presumptive regeneration." Kuyper taught that the covenant warrants the presumption that children of believers are regenerated from earliest infancy and possess saving grace unless they later reject the covenant.

The fruits of presumptive regeneration are often tragic. Parents who presume that their children are regenerate by virtue of the covenant see no need to tell their children that they must be born again and come to repentance and faith in Jesus Christ. William Young calls this view "hyper-covenantism," because the relation of children to the covenant is exaggerated to the point that the covenant relation replaces the need for personal conversion. As Young points out, "Doctrinal knowledge and ethical conduct according to the Word of God are sufficient for the Christian life without any specific religious experience of conviction of sin and conversion, or any need for self-examination as to the possession of distinguishing marks of saving grace."[7]

Consequently, what our Reformed forefathers called experimental religion is deemed largely superfluous. Ultimately, though Kuyperian neo-Calvinists may not like to admit it, religious life becomes grounded in external church institutions and activities rather than in the soul's communion with God. "A system for breeding Pharisees, whose cry is 'We are Abraham's children,' could hardly be better calculated," Young concludes.[8]

---

7. *Westminster Theological Journal* 36, 2 (1974):166.

8. Ibid., 167.

Other Reformed, evangelical churches hold slightly different views of the covenant, such as dormant regeneration or covenantal regeneration. But in practice, these also place too much weight on externals of the covenant. They also minimize the necessity of a new birth, a personal relationship with God, and self-examination in the light of Scripture.

2. They *underestimate* the covenant. Many Baptists and some Reformed people reduce the covenant to insignificance. They do this by failing to recognize the importance of the covenantal relationship of children with God. From the New Testament era on, they believe, children of believers have no promise extended to them, and thus by implication have lost their special place of belonging to the covenant of Jehovah.

Surely this isn't the teaching of the New Testament. Scripturally, the covenant relationship of children to God is established from texts such as Genesis 17:7 ("And I will establish my covenant between me and thee and thy seed after thee in their generations for an everlasting covenant, to be a God unto thee, and to thy seed after thee"), Acts 2:39 ("the promise is unto you, and to your children") and 1 Corinthians 7:14 ("for the unbelieving husband is sanctified by the wife, and the unbelieving wife is sanctified by the husband: else were your children unclean; but now are they holy"). God sovereignly and graciously establishes a redemptive relationship with believers and their offspring. It is unthinkable that in the fullness of the gospel era, the children of the New Testament church would have less of a place in the covenant than children of Old Testament Israel. Practically, Christian parents of the New Testament church who cared deeply about their children would have clamored for clarity on the covenantal position of their children had God really intended them to have no promise, no sacramental sign and seal, and no rightful place among His people.

Some Reformed churches depreciate the covenant relation of children, not by rejecting infant baptism and the covenant relation altogether, but by reducing the sacrament to mere form and custom without insisting on what it should mean for the lives both of the parents and their baptized children. In such circles, the church has no eye for the promises of God in baptism, no heart for pleading those promises in prayer, and no clear understanding of how God earnestly calls covenant children to a lifestyle consecrated to Himself and separated from the world.

Properly Estimating the Covenant

The covenant must be viewed neither as a substitute for regeneration and conversion nor as a matter of secondary importance. The covenantal relationship, which is confirmed in infant baptism, means the following to believing parents:

1. Baptized children must be born again. The Form for the Administration of Baptism tells us, "Our children are conceived and born in sin, and therefore are children of

wrath, insomuch that [they] cannot enter into the kingdom of God except [they] are born again. Our children...
therefore are subject to all miseries, yea to condemnation itself."[9] The Belgic Confession of Faith says:

> We believe that, through the disobedience of
> Adam, original sin is extended to all mankind,
> which is a corruption of the whole nature, and a
> hereditary disease, wherewith infants themselves
> are infected, even in their mother's womb, and
> which produceth in man all sorts of sin, being
> in him as a root thereof; and therefore is so vile
> and abominable in the sight of God that it is suf-
> ficient to condemn all mankind. Nor is it by any
> means abolished or done away by baptism, since
> sin always issues forth from this woeful source as
> water from a fountain.[10]

Baptism, the sign of one's external relationship to
the covenant, is not sufficient for our children's salvation. Baptism affirms that the baptized child is placed
under covenant privileges and responsibilities, but does
not make the child a partaker of the saving, internal
essence of the covenant. The external covenant relationship can be broken when a child grows to adulthood
and abandons God's Word and the corporate worship
of His people. Baptized children must be linked to the
internal, unbreakable essence of the covenant through

---

9. *Doctrinal Standards, Liturgy, and Church Order*, ed. Joel R.
Beeke (Grand Rapids: Reformation Heritage Books, 1999), 126–27.

10. Ibid., 12.

the regenerating work of the Holy Spirit (John 3:3–7). Only then shall they be given persevering grace for the rest of their lives.

Without the Spirit's sovereign, saving work, all our efforts to train our children covenantally will do no more than produce Pharisees on the one hand or rebels on the other. Grace is not automatically conveyed from one generation to another through baptism and faithful covenantal child-rearing. Samuel Rutherford, a Scottish divine who stressed the value of the covenant of grace, wrote, "Grace always runs in the covenant of God, but it does not always run in the blood of the veins." Only the Holy Spirit can bless our efforts and grant our children a broken heart and a contrite spirit (Ps. 51:17).

2. Baptized children must be directed to Jesus Christ and His sacrifice as the only way of salvation. Christ's cleansing blood, symbolized by the cleansing water of baptism, is the only way by which our children may be saved. Baptism teaches us and our children "to loathe and humble ourselves before God, and seek for our purification and salvation without [i.e. outside of] ourselves," the Reformed liturgy says.[11] Question 72 of the Heidelberg Catechism says, "Is then the external baptism with water the washing away of sin itself? Not at all; for the blood of Jesus Christ only, and the Holy Ghost cleanse us from all sin" (Matt. 3:11; 1 John 1:7).

---

11. Ibid., 126.

3. Baptism demands new, heartfelt obedience to God. As the Dutch Reformed liturgy says, a true covenantal relationship with God requires repentance and love toward God, faith toward our Lord Jesus Christ, and a lifestyle of separation whereby "we forsake the world, crucify our old nature, and walk in a new and holy life."[12] We must teach our children that they are not allowed to bring their "baptized foreheads" into ungodly places, to bond with ungodly people, or engage in ungodly activities.

We must also teach our children that being outwardly good and obedient falls short of their covenantal obligation to God. We must shepherd their hearts, teaching them daily by our words and example that they are called to holiness of heart and holiness of life. Paul tells us in 1 Timothy 4:4–5 that everything is to be sanctified. The call to holiness is an absolute, comprehensive, and exclusive call involving separation from sin and consecration to God from the heart. "My son, give me thine heart" (Prov. 23:26).[13]

4. Baptism requires parents to instruct their children in the Christian faith and the doctrine of salvation (see Q. 3 of the Form of Baptism). Numerous texts make the instruction of children the primary responsibility

---

12. Ibid.

13. See Tedd Tripp, *Shepherding a Child's Heart* (Wapwallopen, Penn.: Shepherd Press, 1995), 3–7; Joel R. Beeke, *Holiness: God's Call to Sanctification* (Edinburgh: Banner of Truth Trust, 1994), 6–7.

of the church's parents (Ex. 12:24–27; Deut. 6:4–9; 2 Tim. 3:14–15).

Children are entrusted to us with the divine command that we are not to provoke them to wrath but to "bring them up in the nurture and admonition of the Lord" (Eph. 6:4). We are not to raise them according to our own ideas of nurture and admonition but according to "the nurture and admonition of the Lord." God says that we must train our children in every respect—spiritually, morally, socially, emotionally, and physically—on His behalf and according to His Word.

The entire book of Proverbs illustrates the manner and substance of parental covenantal nurture. The covenant home must be a temple in which God is acknowledged and worshiped (2 Sam. 6:20; Pss. 34:11–14; 90:16; 105:5–6; 118:15; 132:12; 147:13).[14]

5. Baptism teaches that God, in and through the Second Adam, Jesus Christ, is able and willing to be the Redeemer and Father of our children. "As they are without their knowledge partakers of the condemnation in Adam, so are they again received unto grace in Christ," the Form concludes.[15] Our children are Christ's covenant seed (Ps. 22:30; Isa. 53:10). He calls them "an heritage of the LORD" (Ps. 127:3). They belong to Him. He has a claim upon them, even in their unregenerate

---

14. Cf. Douglas Wilson, *Standing on the Promises: A Handbook of Biblical Childrearing* (Moscow, Idaho: Canon Press, 1997), esp. chapters 1, 4, 5.

15. *Doctrinal Standards*, 126.

state, just as He had a claim upon all the children of Israel, calling them His even when many were not truly born again (Ezek. 16:20–21).

6. God ordinarily works savingly among His covenant seed. Among the unchurched and uncovenanted, God occasionally draws children to salvation in Christ. Sunday schools and other evangelistic outreaches have been particularly helpful in this respect. As Psalm 68:5–6 says, God is "a father of the fatherless.... God setteth the solitary in families." But among His covenant people, His saving grace is the norm, due to His amazing covenantal love and His blessing upon faithful parenting. As Herman Witsius wrote:

> Here certainly appears the extraordinary love of our God, in that as soon as we are born, and just as we come from our mother, he hath commanded us to be solemnly brought from her bosom, as it were into his own arms, that he should bestow upon us, in the very cradle, the tokens of our dignity and future kingdom; that he should put that song in our mouth, "Thou didst make me hope when I was upon my mother's breast: I was cast upon thee from the womb: thou art my God from my mother's belly" (Ps. 22:9–10), that, in a word, he should join us to himself in the most solemn covenant from our most tender years: the remembrance of which, as it is glorious and full of consolation to us, so in like manner it tends to

promote Christian virtues, and the strictest holiness, through the whole course of our lives.[16]

The covenant creates the context in which we make diligent use of the means of grace, and we believe that the God of the covenant often honors such use of His ordained means, though, being the sovereign Jehovah, He is by no means obliged to do so (Rom. 9:11–13). Nevertheless, Scripture affirms that the Holy Spirit richly blesses the evangelizing and nurturing of covenant children in knowledge, faith, love, and obedience (Gen. 18:19; Prov. 22:6). Faithful parenting, by the Spirit's blessing, frequently issues in regeneration and a life of covenantal faithfulness (Ps. 78:1–8).[17]

Knowing such things should encourage us more to evangelize our children and to plead for their salvation, never giving God rest until they are all brought safely into His fold. Then, too, we must teach our covenant children and young people to plead with our covenant God on the basis of His promises to baptize them with the Spirit of grace and to grant them regeneration, repentance, and faith.

---

16. *The Economy of the Covenants Between God and Man* (Grand Rapids: Reformation Heritage Books, 2010), 2:442.

17. See Richard Baxter, *A Christian Directory* (Grand Rapids: Soli Deo Gloria, 2008), 409–31, 449–54; Thomas Manton, *The Complete Works* (Worthington, Penn.: Maranatha, n.d.), 15:463–74; William Guthrie, *The Christian's Great Interest* (Edinburgh: Banner of Truth Trust, 1993), 38–39: Jacobus Koelman, *The Duties of Parents* (Grand Rapids: Reformation Heritage Books, 2009), chapter 4.

7. We can expect great things from a covenant-keeping God. Malachi 2:15 stresses that God desires a godly seed and Psalm 103:17 promises His mercy and righteousness to children's children.

Scripture offers many examples of God-fearing children. Exodus 20:6 affirms in Hebrew that God shows mercy unto "thousands of generations" that love Him and keep His commandments.[18] The evangelization and nurture of the church's children has been one of the greatest means of church growth ever since the church's beginning in Eden.

Church history also confirms God's faithfulness to His covenant children, shown by the God-honoring fruits in their lives. Thomas Boston, Matthew Henry, William Carey, David Livingstone, and John Paton were all the products of godly homes. Godly lines of succession, as can be found in the Edwards, Mather, and Hodge families in America, can easily be multiplied.[19]

---

18. See Jonathan Neil Gerstner, *The Thousand Generation Covenant: Dutch Reformed Covenant Theology and Group Identity in Colonial South Africa, 1652–1814* (Leiden: Brill, 1991).

19. L. H. Atwater, "The Children of the Church and Sealing Ordinances," *Biblical Repertory and Princeton Review* 29, 1 (1857): 13–16; Lewis Bevens Schenck, *The Presbyterian Doctrine of Children in the Covenant: An Historical Study of the Significance of Infant Baptism in the Presbyterian Church in America* (New Haven, Conn.: Yale, 1940); D. Jones, "The Doctrine of the Church in American Presbyterian Theology in the Mid-Nineteenth Century" (Th.D. dissertation, Concordia Seminary, 1970), 49–86; Peter Masters and Malcolm H. Watts, *The Necessity of Sunday Schools* (London: Wakeman Trust, 1992), chapter 6; Robert S. Rayburn,

We do not expect children to act like adults, however (1 Cor. 13:11). Their spiritual experiences will usually be commensurate with their age, but the same fruits of grace—such as hatred for sin, love for Christ, and yearnings for holiness—that are evident in adults will be evident in them.[20]

Covenant theology does not negate the need for us to evangelize our children, nor does it discourage us from doing so. Scripture offers no guarantees for the salvation of our children, but the covenant of grace offers us a great deal of hope outside of ourselves in a sovereign, covenant-keeping God, who will not forsake the works of His own hands (Ps. 138:8). Covenant theology should encourage us to evangelize our children as we daily, prayerfully, and expectantly depend upon the triune God for His blessing upon our efforts.[21]

We cannot take this encouragement for granted, however. No matter how well you teach, train, and model godly living for your children, God is still sovereign and He rules (Isa. 14:27; 46:10; Rom. 9:11–13; Eph. 1:5–9). We must rest in the triune God who declares that all things are "of him, and through him, and to him" (Rom. 11:36), then trust that the Holy

---

"The Presbyterian Doctrines of Covenant Children, Covenant Nurture, and Covenant Succession," *Presbyterion* 22 (1996):95–96.

20. Cf. Archibald Alexander, *Thoughts on Religious Experience* (Edinburgh: Banner of Truth Trust reprint, 1975), 11–20.

21. *The Collected Writings of James Henley Thornwell* (Edinburgh: Banner of Truth Trust reprint), 4:340; Sisemore, 66–68.

Spirit is able and willing to sovereignly and graciously convert covenant children.

If God commanded that children hear the gospel repeatedly throughout the Old Testament era (Ex. 12:25–27; Deut. 30:19; Josh. 4:21–24), shouldn't we also tell the gospel to our children in the fullness of the New Testament age? If Christ commands the church to go into all the world and preach the gospel to every creature (Mark 16:15), shouldn't we also evangelize our covenant children? If Paul used every opportunity to carry the gospel to people all around the world, shouldn't we seize every opportunity to evangelize our own children (Acts 20:1–16)? If Paul felt it was his duty to bring the gospel to all men, making himself a servant to all (1 Cor. 19:19–22), shouldn't we become servants of the gospel to our own children to evangelize them?[22]

We may never opt out of our covenant responsibility to evangelize our children. Deuteronomy 6:7 says that we must teach God's Word to our children "diligently," that is, with steady, earnest attention, and energetic application and effort. Psalm 78:4–7 says, for God's covenant sake we are to show "to the generation to come the praises of the LORD, and his strength, and his wonderful works that he hath done, [so] that the generation to come might know them,…might set their hope in God, and not forget the works of God, but keep his commandments" (cf. Pss. 71:17–18; 145:4).

---

22. Ibid., chapter 5.

Teaching the Content of the Gospel ☐2

Your task is to teach your children the whole gospel and counsel of God, as Paul said he did for the Ephesians (Acts 20:17–27). Fathers, you especially are to be ministers in your own houses. Your home is a little church, a little seminary, in which together with your wife, you are to serve as an instructing prophet, an interceding priest, and a guiding king. As a prophet, you must teach your children God's truth, addressing the mind, the conscience, the heart, and the will. That means you must teach your children Bible stories and Bible doctrines, and you must apply those stories and doctrines to their daily lives for their proper development—spiritually, morally, socially, emotionally, and physically.

You must also explain how God's truth is experienced by His people—that is, how matters should and do go in the lives of those who know God in Jesus Christ. Aim to apply divine truth to the whole range of your children's experience. Teach them how God's people repeatedly experience the depths of their sin and misery, the fullness of deliverance in Jesus Christ, and the magnitude of gratitude to God for such deliverance. All of this is to be done in the context of biblical piety.

You may feel that this task overwhelms you. "Exactly how do I communicate these truths to my children?" you ask. "I am confused and nervous, even afraid, to speak to them about God and salvation. I've never done it before—certainly not adequately. How should I impress the claims of the gospel upon my children?"

In evangelizing your children, it is helpful to break down your task into specific doctrines. Here are some specific doctrines you should stress with your children, if you would bring them God's whole counsel:

1. Teach them who God is and what He is like. Use the Scriptures and the Psalter to proclaim God's majestic sovereignty, His triune personality, and His glorious attributes to your children. Study Psalm 139, Isaiah 6, Isaiah 40, John 1, and Ephesians 1 with them. Root the evangelizing of them in a robust biblical theism rather than that of modern evangelicalism, which treats God as if He were a next-door neighbor who can adjust His attributes to our needs and desires.

Tell your children about the sovereign, holy character of God—that He cannot forgive sin "without the shedding of blood," for "the wages of sin is death" (Rom. 6:23). Tell them about God's righteous judgment and holy wrath against all ungodliness and unrighteousness of men. Tell them that God hates sin and demands that parents punish sin in their children because it is God's will that sin be punished. Tell your children how you as parents are to exhibit the character of God even though you, too, are sinners and need God's grace to do that. Ask them to pray for you so you may model the character of God in the Lord Jesus Christ.

2. Teach them the seriousness of sin. You must show your children that they have a heart problem because of the Fall. Teach them, as the New England Primer said: "In Adam's fall, we sinned all." Explain to them at a level they can understand the great truths of Genesis 2 and 3: that God created us perfect, after His image in knowledge, righteousness, and holiness. Teach them that Adam represented us in Paradise and how we fell in and with him so that we have become selfish, proud, and wicked. His sin has now become our sin; it is our state and condition, and it causes death. Tell them that is why we must all die.

The idea of total depravity and misery is helpful to use as a starting point in explaining Reformed, experiential truth. Illustrate for them how bad we are by nature. For example, show them a cup that is white on the outside and black on the inside. Tell them that is much like us — we can appear quite pure in our behavior but are black with corruption within. We are all conceived and born in sin (Ps. 51:5).

Teach them also that we have the problem of a bad record and are all lawbreakers. Explain that because we are sinners we commit a host of sins in thought, word, and deed. Call sin, sin. Tell them, lovingly yet firmly, that no one had to teach them how to sin — to become angry, to disobey, to be selfish, or to be jealous—because by nature we are all sinful. Explain how their first acts showed sin. When you must discipline them, remind them that the sins they commit flow from their corrupt, sinful hearts.

Stress the sinfulness of sin. Read and talk about Romans 3:9–20 with your children. Explain how sin is disobedience to God and how it grieves Him and cuts us off from Him. Explain that the least sin involves more evil than the greatest affliction and that sin is the poison that makes us comfortable with the ungodly world and with Satan. Aim to convict them of sin and to foster a due sense of the fear of God by addressing their consciences, even as you realize that the Holy Spirit alone, through irresistible grace, can bless your efforts by truly convicting them of sin and leading them to a childlike fear of God.

3. Teach them what the Bible says about unrepentant sin. Teach them that sin is moral rebellion against God, and that those who persist in it will reap eternal condemnation. Teach them about hell to create within them, by the blessing of the Spirit, a sense of need for Jesus Christ. Use Christ's teaching on the tares and wheat, or on the abuse of talents (Matt. 13:30–50; 25:28–46), to describe hell as a place devoid of God's favor and blessing. Concentrate more on the essence of hell than on its vivid details.

Children must know that they are in danger of hell and that it is a dreadful place where sinners will be left in sin without any hope of forgiveness. Children are not served by blinding their eyes to this truth. You must teach them this as lovingly and soberly as you can, praying they will repent of their sin before God and believe in Christ alone for salvation.

Don't be afraid to talk to your children about hell, as that can make a deep impression upon them. They can become very silent when you speak to them about hell. But that knowledge is an important evangelistic tool in your arsenal of truth — a tool that the Holy Spirit has used throughout church history to show His children that they need to forsake sin and flee from the wrath of God to the cleansing blood of Jesus Christ.[1]

4. Teach them they must be born again (Ps. 51:6, 7, 10; John 3:3 – 5). The nature and consequences of sin are the same for children as for adults. Children must be taught that their bad hearts and bad records make them unfit for communion with God. Do not dismiss your children's sins as mere naughtiness or childish behavior. Don't excuse their sins by repeating clichés such as, "Boys will be boys." And never encourage them to feel that being outwardly good is sufficient in God's eyes.

More than good behavior is needed to meet the demands of God; inward regeneration of heart through a triune God is essential for salvation, as Christ stressed with Nicodemus (John 3:3 –7). Our children are not

---

1. R. Hudson Pope and A. C. Capon, *Know How to Evangelize Your Children* (London: Scripture Union, 1962), 7 – 8.

merely sick and in need of reformation; they are born
dead in trespasses and sins and need regeneration (Ps.
51:5; Eph. 2:1). Explain to young children the difference
between a physical heart and a spiritual heart, and set
before them the basic marks of grace.[2] In elementary
school years, explain to them that Christ was addressing Nicodemus as a "master in Israel," and therefore
he was externally in covenant with God, yet Christ
tells him that he and the people he represents must be
born again. Point out to them the plural in the state-
ment, "Ye must be born again," and stress that this still
applies to them today. As teenagers, explain the biblical
appeal regarding the need for "circumcision in heart"
(Deut. 10:6; 30:6; Jer. 4:4; Rom. 2:25–29; Col. 2:11).
Expound Paul's description of the true Israelite as "the
true circumcision" (Phil. 3:3), and compare that with
Christ's desciption of Nathaniel in John 1:47. Study
with them Paul's definition of the true seed of Abraham
in Romans 4:11–12 and Galatians 3.

Impress these truths in every way you can, appropriate to their age. Pray for wisdom to teach clearly and
for grace to feel deeply your children's inability to do
anything toward their salvation while refusing, at the
same time, to shirk your responsibility because of their
inability. Cling to the hope that there is more goodness
and ability in God than badness and inability in your chil-

2. Joel R. Beeke and Heidi Boorsma, *God's Alphabet for
Life: Devotions for Young Children,* 2nd ed. (Grand Rapids:
Reformation Heritage Books, 2009), 10–12.

dren, that God's grace supersedes their wretchedness and hell-worthiness. As Samuel Bolton said, "There is more goodness in God than evil in ten thousand hells of sin."

5. Teach them about the moral law and its uses:

- *The civil use.* Explain how God uses the law in public life to guide the civil magistrate as he rewards good, punishes evil, and restrains sin (Rom. 13:3–4). Teach them that the law is a reliable standard of right and wrong, good and evil, for the home and family life as well, and that we as parents must use the law to promote righteousness and to restrain wickedness. Just as society would lapse into anarchy without the enforcement of God's moral law, so our homes would lapse into chaos without the Ten Commandments being strictly enjoined. We need this first use of the law to regulate the life of the home.

- *The evangelical use.* Explain to your children how the law, wielded by the Spirit of God, serves a critical function in the experience of conversion. It accuses, convicts, and condemns. It exposes our sinfulness, strips us of all our righteousness, condemns us, pronounces a curse upon us, and knows no mercy. It declares us liable to the wrath of God and the torments of hell. Galatians 3:10 says, "Cursed is every one that continueth not in all things which are written in the book of the law to do them." But the law does all this to drive us to the end of the law, Christ Jesus, who is our only acceptable righteousness before God (Gal. 3:24). Teach your children that the Holy Spirit uses the law as a mirror to show us our impotence and our guilt, to shut us up to hope in mercy alone, and to induce repentance, creating and sustaining the sense of spiritual need out of which faith in Christ is born.

- *The didactic use.* Teach your children that when a sinner is saved, he still needs the law as a rule of life. God uses the moral law to sanctify believers in their daily walk of life. Show them from the Heidelberg Catechism the difference between the convicting, evangelical use of the law (Lord's Day 2) and the didactic use of the law that promotes thankfulness (Lord's Days 34–44). One way of teaching young children this difference is to explain Luther's assertion that the law is like a "stick"—the Holy Spirit first uses it as a rod to beat a sinner to Christ, then, after conversion, as a cane to assist a believer in walking as a follower of Christ.

    Show your older children from the Psalms, the Sermon on the Mount, and the ethical portions of Paul's epistles that believers relish the law as a rule of life (see especially Psalm 119). Explain to teenagers how walking in accord with God's law keeps believers from antinomianism (*anti* = against; *nomos* = law; i.e., being against the law) on the one hand, and legalism on the other. Show them how obedience to God's law promotes brotherly love (1 John 5:3) and authentic Christian freedom (Ps. 116).[3]

6. Teach them that the atoning blood of Jesus Christ is the only way of salvation. Again and again, explain to your children the basics of the gospel: how Jesus saves sinners through His suffering, death, resurrection, and life. Use especially the book of Romans, notable chapters such as Isaiah 53 and 1 Corinthians 15, and individual verses such as 2 Corinthians 5:21 and 1 John 1:9. Use illustrations to explain the principle of substitution. Here is one that I use for young children:

One day Tom's class had a substitute teacher. His friend, George, who was handicapped, disobeyed the teacher. The teacher ordered George to stand in the corner with his face to the wall. She didn't know that George couldn't stand because of his weak legs. So Tom raised his hand. When the teacher called on him, Tom asked, "May I stand in the corner for George?"

Surprised, the teacher asked, "Why would you want to do that, Tom?"

"George can't do it," Tom said, "so I want to take his place."

The teacher let Tom stand in for George. Then the teacher told the class, "That's what Jesus does for sinners like us. We have all been disobedient. Every time

---

3. Joel Beeke and Ray Lanning, "Glad Obedience," in *Trust and Obey*, ed. Don Kistler (Morgan, Penn.: Soli Deo Gloria, 1996), 188–95.

we are disobedient we sin. We deserve to stand in the corner of God's anger and wrath. But we can't stand in the face of God's anger. His anger is too great against sin, and we are too weak to stand. So, out of His great heart of grace and love, God sent His Son to stand in the corner to bear the sins of sinners like us. Jesus did that when He suffered in the Garden of Gethsemane and especially when He died on Calvary's cross. He didn't suffer and die for Himself but for people like George, and you, and me, who can't stand in the corner of God's wrath. Just as I am letting George go free for Tom's sake because he is taking George's place, so God lets sinners who believe in Jesus alone for salvation go free because Jesus takes their place."

Use Scripture and illustrations to explain the basics of the gospel. Tell your children why Jesus had to obey the law perfectly, pointing out that we cannot do so by nature, and why He had to pay for sin to satisfy the justice of God. Stress that the cross and salvation flow from the Father's love and that all the persons of the Holy Trinity delight to save sinners.

7. Teach them the necessity of faith in Jesus Christ. Walk them through John 3, and stress verse 36, "He that believeth on the Son hath everlasting life: and he that believeth not the Son shall not see life; but the wrath of God abideth on him." Teach them that the gospel is one thing and our response to it is another. Tell them they must believe in Jesus Christ alone for salvation by Spirit-worked faith.

Show them illustrations of the trusting character of faith, such as this story: A famous minister from Scotland, Thomas Chalmers, once talked to an elderly woman for hours about her need to believe in Jesus Christ. She kept insisting that she didn't dare believe. She was afraid that she, rather than God, would be saving herself if she believed. Chalmers couldn't get her to understand the nature of faith as God's gracious gift and left quite discouraged.

To return home, Chalmers had to walk over a sturdy bridge that spanned a small stream in the woman's yard. As he approached the bridge, Chalmers stood back, looked at it suspiciously, then touched it with his fingers. Then he jumped back in fear.

The woman, watching from her window, was astonished. After Chalmers repeated the act a few times, the woman shouted, "Lippen till it! Lippen till it!," an old Scottish expression meaning, "Trust in it," or "Depend on it."

Chalmers shouted back, "Depend on Jesus Christ. He's as safe as this bridge. He'll bring you across!"

The woman's eyes were opened. She had not questioned Christ's trustworthiness, but now she saw the gospel warrant to believe. By grace, she trusted in Christ—and Him alone—for salvation. She believed and was saved.

In addition to explaining what faith is, explain to your children what saving faith does, using chapters such as Romans 3 and 4, Galatians 3, Hebrews 4 and 11, and James 2. Teach them how faith wholeheartedly assents to the truth of the gospel and falls into the out-stretched arms of God. Tell how it flees in poverty to Christ's riches; in guilt to Christ's reconciliation; in bondage to Christ's liberation. Tell how it lays hold of Christ and His righteousness, uniting the sinner with the Savior. Tell how it embraces Christ in belief, clinging to His Word and relying on His promises. As Luther wrote, "Faith clasps Christ as a ring clasps its jewel." Faith wraps the soul in Christ's righteousness, then lives out of Christ. Faith commits the total person to the total Christ.

Show them from Ephesians 2 that faith and grace are not competitors, that salvation is through faith because only in faith is divine grace honored. Invite them to flee to Jesus and to respond to the gospel in faith, but don't put all the stress on the will. Tell them they have a duty to repent, not just as a temporary feeling of sorrow, but as a full amendment of life.[4]

Then, too, urge them to "cease to do evil; learn to do well" (Isa. 1:16–17) and to be holy as God is holy. Call them to love God and His holy law with heart and mind and strength, and to let nothing stand in the way of obedience. Plead with them to seek the Lord while He is near and to "strive to enter in at the strait gate" (Luke 13:24).[5] Tell them to do this now, lest they be in

---

4. Joel R. Beeke, "The Relation of Faith to Justification," in *Justification by Faith Alone*, ed. Don Kistler (Morgan, Penn.: Soli Deo Gloria, 1995), 68–77.

5. Joel R. Beeke, *Puritan Evangelism: A Biblical Approach,* 2nd ed. (Grand Rapids: Reformation Heritage Books, 1999), 34–35.

danger of hardening. Tell them they must remember their Creator now in the days of their youth (Eccl. 12:1).

8. Teach them about Jesus Christ. Do what Jesus did on the road to Emmaus: begin at Moses and the prophets, and expound to them in all the Scriptures the truths concerning Jesus Christ.

Present the whole Christ to your child. Tell the child who Christ is, what He has done on Calvary, and what He is doing now at the right hand of the Father. Use Philippians 2:5–11 to explain His states and natures. Offer Him as prophet, priest, and king. Do not separate His benefits from His person or offer Him as a Savior from sin while ignoring His claims as Lord. Speak of Him winsomely. Speak of His preciousness, His ability, His willingness to save children. Extol Christ. Explain how He is altogether lovely for needy sinners (Song 5:16). Tell them what you find in Him—that for you to live is Christ and to die is gain (Phil. 1:21).

Strive to develop a biblical, Christ-centered worldview in your children. Teach them that every thought must be brought into captivity to the obedience of Christ (2 Cor. 10:5). Assist them in setting Christ at the center of every subject and every sphere of life. Help them to see that in Christ, the precious Redeemer and sovereign King, all of life's issues meet. He is Lord of all and will put all things under His feet (1 Cor. 15:24–25). To Him is all power and authority given in heaven and earth (Matt. 28:18).

9. Teach them about sanctification and holiness. Talk to your children about the fruits of grace that are evident in the lives of children who are born again. Teach them that redeemed children will hate sin, fear God, love Jesus, and long to be holy. Show them from the Bible that holiness will become visible in such children through their gratitude, service, prayer, obedience, love, and self-denial. Go through the Beatitudes (Matt. 5:3–12) and Paul's list of the Spirit's fruits (Gal. 5:22–23).

Teach them that God's children will love the things of God: His Word, His Sabbath day, and His people. They will covenant their lives back to God by surrendering and consecrating all that they are and have to God and His kingdom (Matt. 6:33).

Explain to them various inducements to holiness, such as:

- God calls us to holiness for our good and His glory (1 Thess. 4:7)

- Holiness makes us resemble Christ and preserves integrity (Phil. 2:5–13)

- Holiness gives evidence of justification and election, and fosters assurance (1 Cor. 6:11; 2 Thess. 2:13; 1 John 2:3)

- Holiness alone can purify us (Tit. 1:15)

- Holiness is essential for effective service to God (2 Tim. 2:21)

- Holiness fits us for heaven (Heb. 12:14; Rev. 21:27)

10. Teach them about the joy of heaven. Focus on the blessedness of being with God, the holy angels, and all the redeemed, and of the believer finally becoming what he has desired to be ever since his regeneration — perfectly holy in a Triune God, a son of God and fellow-heir with Christ (Phil. 3:20–21; Rom. 8:17). Explain from Hebrews 12:1–2 how Jesus was motivated to endure His sufferings by anticipating the joy of His reward. Let your children see how you long for the day when Jesus Christ returns to establish a new heaven and a new earth (2 Peter 3:13–14).

In all your teaching, be reverent and serious, yet natural. Let your children feel that what you speak is real. Look them straight in the eye as you speak. Show your love for their souls. Don't be afraid to weep as you speak of the loveliness of Christ or warn them to flee from the wrath to come. Do not joke with your children about any Bible truth, Bible character, or Bible instruction. Do not make light of the things of God. Life is too serious, death too final, judgment too certain, and eternity too long to indulge in humor about the sacred truths of Scripture.

Using the Means $\boxed{3}$

Once you have explained the gospel content to your children, how do you use that to confront your children with the claims of the gospel?

You must first realize as parents that you are primarily responsible for the evangelism of your children. Practically speaking, that means making sure that any person, institution, or thing that has regular influence over your child for any length of time — be that a church and its office-bearers, a school and its teachers, a babysitter, or the high-tech world of computers — has the same Bible-centered, Christ-honoring worldlife view that you have.

Children need consistency, particularly in the three major sources of input in their lives: home, church, and school. These three form a triangle, and we as parents are responsible for all three. For now, let's examine our responsibility in the home.

A godly home is the greatest context of evangelism for children. It involves these ingredients:

Prayer

"A family without prayer is like a house without a roof, open and exposed to all the storms of heaven," said Thomas Brooks. We need to pray for and with our children. Specifically, we must pray:

1. *Habitually.* Designate a time and place for prayer in your daily schedule, and place children at the top of the list. Prayer is the first and best thing we can do for our children. "You can do more than pray after you have prayed, but you can't do more than pray until you have prayed," John Bunyan wrote.

2. *Spontaneously.* Whenever we feel the need to pray for a child, we ought to pray immediately. Our Dutch forebears called that "hat-on" praying, meaning literally to pray with one's hat on, offering short, pungent petitions while driving, ironing, studying, or doing anything else. If we hesitate when we receive such impulses, the urge to pray will be greatly diminished.

3. *Covenantally.* We must pray for our children, pleading upon their covenant relationship with God. God has placed His name beside theirs in baptism and claimed them as His. Show Him the baptized foreheads of your children. Like David, plead, "Have respect unto [thy] covenant" (Ps. 74:20), for Thy glory's sake.

4. *Specifically.* Our prayers are often riddled with clichés. Our children need deliberate, specific petitions that wage war against the hostile culture of our day,

which competes for their souls. Praying for each child's specific needs should be done individually by each parent, but also together. We must pray for conversion, for saving faith, and for preserving grace for each child. We must pray for the daily assaults and struggles to which our precious children are subject.

For believing children, we should pray through the Beatitudes and the passages on the fruits of the Spirit. We should pray that these children's minds will be filled with the good things of Philippians 4:8 and that their wills may be fenced in by the Ten Commandments.

We must pray for ourselves as parents, too, asking for strength for specific tasks, wisdom to make good decisions, and for patience and endurance in the ongoing task of parenting.

5. *Earnestly*. Prayer is our greatest weapon in raising a Christian family. As the old saying goes, "The devil trembles when he sees the weakest saint upon his knees."

Let's seek grace to pray as Alexander Whyte did for his children:

O Almighty God, our Heavenly Father, give us a seed right with Thee! Smite us and our house with everlasting barrenness rather than that our seed should not be right with Thee. O God, give us our children. Give us our children. A second time, and by a far better birth, give us our children to be beside us in Thy holy covenant. For it had been better we had never been betrothed; it had been better we had sat all our days solitary unless our children are to be right with Thee.... But thou, O

God, art Thyself a Father, and thus hast in Thyself
a Father's heart. Hear us, then, for our children,
O our Father.... In season and out of season, we
shall not go up into our bed, we shall not give
sleep to our eyes nor slumber to our eyelids till we
and all our seed are right with Thee.[1]

Charles Spurgeon once wrote, "How can a man be a
Christian, and not love his offspring? How can a man
be a believer in Jesus Christ, and yet have a cold and
hard heart in the things of the kingdom towards his
children?... It is our business to train up our children
in the fear of the Lord; and though we cannot give them
grace, it is ours to pray to the God who can give it; and
in answer to our many supplications, he will not turn us
away, but will be pleased to regard our sighs."[2]

Spurgeon's mother was one who prayed this way.
Spurgeon remembered sitting on her lap and feeling
her warm tears as she prayed, "Lord, Thou knowest if
these prayers are not answered in Charles's conversion,
these very petitions will have to bear witness against
him in the day of judgment."

The lesson was not lost on her son. "The thought
that my mother's prayers would serve as witness against
me in the day of judgment sent terror into my heart,"
Spurgeon later wrote.

---

1. Alexander Whyte, *Bunyan Characters* (London: Pickering &
Inglis, 1902), 3:289–90.

2. *20 Centuries of Great Preaching*, ed. Clyde E. Fant, Jr.
(Waco, Tex.: Word Books, 1971), 6:93–94.

Seek grace by prayer to bring the benediction of Almighty God upon your household (Matt. 11:12). Pray earnestly, remembering God's rich promises to answer prayer (Isa. 30:18–19; Matt. 7:7–8; John 16:23–24). Rely on God's sympathetic ear (Heb. 11:6). Pray with faith and persistence (James 1:5–7; Luke 18:1), according to God's will (1 John 5:14–15), trusting that God will answer in His time. As John Witherspoon, the only minister to sign the Declaration of Independence, wrote: "I could tell you some remarkable instances of parents who seemed to labor in vain for a long time, and yet were so happy as to see a change at last; and of some children in whom even after the death of the parents, the seed which was early sown, and seemed to have been entirely smothered, has at last produced fruit."[3]

Jeremiah 10:25 warns us that God will pour out His fury upon families who do not call upon His name. But blessed are those children who can later say, "The prayers of my God-fearing father and mother kept me from much sin and led me to the Lord Jesus Christ."

Family Worship

Like Abraham, lovingly but firmly command your household to worship God (Gen. 18:19). Be determined, like Joshua, to serve and worship God daily in your family (Josh. 24:15). As head of the household, gather your family at least once a day for Scripture reading, biblical

3. *The Works of John Witherspoon* (Edinburgh: Ogle & Aikman, 1804), 3:499–500.

instruction, prayer, and singing. Here are some helps on how to implement these four aspects of family worship:

1. *Scripture reading.* First, have a plan. For example, read 10–20 verses from the Old Testament in the morning, and from the New Testament in the evening. Or read through the Psalms, then a series of biographical portions. Or read the miracles and parables of Christ. Whatever plan you have, be sure to read the entire Bible with your family over a period of a year or two. Give your children the whole Bible, even while they are young.

Second, take into account special occasions. On Sunday mornings, you might want to read Psalms 48, 63, 84, 92, 118, or John 20. On a Sabbath when the Lord's Supper is being administered, read Psalm 22, Isaiah 53, Matthew 26, or John 6. Or, you may want to read appropriate portions for such special days as Christmas, New Year's Eve, New Year's Day, Easter, Pentecost, etc. When you embark on a trip, read Psalms 91 or 121 together.

Third, involve the family. Let everyone who can read have a Bible in front of them. As head of the household, assign portions for the children to read, too. Teach them to read reverently, slowly, and with expression. Provide a brief word of explanation when needed before, during, or after the reading.

2. *Biblical instruction.* When you teach, be pure in doctrine (Titus 2:7). Don't abandon doctrinal precision when teaching even young children. Aim for simplicity and soundness.

Major on the basics. Teach your children the Ten Commandments, the Lord's Prayer, and the Apostles' Creed as a preparation for further instruction. Repeat them aloud as a family periodically in family worship. Or, use books to assist you, such as plain Bible expositions (e.g., Ryle's *Expository Thoughs on the Gospels,* 7 vols.), Bible stories (e.g., VanDam, MacKenzie, Vos, Vreugdenhil), daily devotionals (e.g., Hawker, Spurgeon, Jay, Mason, Gurnall, M'Cheyne), or stories of God at work in church history (e.g., *Building on the Rock*, 5 vols.).[4]

Be plain in meaning and style. Encourage questions. Draw them out. Ask your children questions appropriate to their varying ages. Have one or two good commentaries on hand as a family, such as those of John Calvin, Matthew Henry, Matthew Poole, and John Gill, to assist the entire family in understanding various texts.

Be experiential and relevant in application. Bring in the soul's experience of the truths you are teaching. Don't be afraid to share your own experiences, but do so simply.

Be affectionate in manner. Proverbs sets the tone for you with its warm, "My son...." Proverbs shows

---

4. These books, and many more helpful for family worship, may be ordered at discount prices from Reformation Heritage Books, 2965 Leonard NE, Grand Rapids, MI 49525 (heritagebooks.org). For more detailed guidelines, see James W. Alexander, *Family Worship* (Morgan, Penn.: Soli Deo Gloria reprint, 1998); Joel R. Beeke, *Family Worship,* 2nd ed. (Grand Rapids: Reformation Heritage Books, 2009); and Terry L. Johnson, ed., *The Family Worship Book: A Resource Book for Family Devotions* (Fearn, Ross-shire: Christian Focus, 1998).

warmth, love, concern, and urgency pulsating in the heart and exhortations of the father.

Reach down into the world of your children. Use concrete, not abstract, concepts. Simplify sermons you've heard for them. Try to tie in biblical instruction as much as possible with current events in the family, society, or nation.

Require your children's full attention. God's truths demand a hearing. You have matters of life and death and eternity to convey. Carry out Proverbs 4:1, "Hear, ye children, the instruction of a father, and attend to know understanding." At times, you may need to say and enforce, "Sit up, son, and look at me while I'm speaking. We're talking about God and His Word, and He deserves to be heard."

3. *Prayer*. Be plain without becoming shallow, be natural and yet solemn, be direct yet varied. Come before God with adoration and dependence as a family. Invoke him properly, making mention of His name, and perhaps one or two of His attributes. Confess family sins and ask for forgiveness for every transgression of the day. Plead for temporal, spiritual, and eternal mercies. Intercede for family friends. Offer thanksgiving for mercies already received. Conclude by blessing God for what He is in Himself and for what He has done for your family. Express the wish that His glory may forever continue. Conclude with a final plea for pardon for the sake of His Son.

4. *Singing.* Introduce your children to the songs of Zion. The Psalms speak to the heart of every believer and cover the whole range of Christian experience. Buy copies of *The Psalter* for every member of the family.[5] Stress those songs that emphasize core truths of the gospel, and that are rich for devotion, instruction, or admonition. For little children, begin with a stanza or two from simpler texts such as numbers 7, 10, 24, 49, 53, 140, 162, 203, 235, 246, 268, 281, 322, 345, 370, 394, 408, and 431. Later, teach them songs that address the problem of sin such as numbers 83, 110, 141-144, 217, and 362, and songs that are full of Christ's person and work, such as numbers 3, 28, 47, 125, 183, 200, 303, 318, 368, 399, and 426. Make frequent use of doxologies, such as numbers 196, 197, 315, 413, and 420:5.

Sing family favorites, but introduce new songs from time to time. Reinforce what is being taught in school or catechism class by using *Psalter* selections assigned for memory work. Encourage habits of good singing such as good posture, proper use of the voice, and clear diction.

Remind your children that they are singing portions of God's Word which should be handled with reverence and care. Pray with them for grace in the heart so that they may sing to the Lord as He commands in His Word (Col. 3:16). Meditate together on the words you sing.

Let your family worship be regular and sincere. As Richard Cecil said, "Let family worship be short,

---

5. *The Psalter* is available from Reformation Heritage Books.

savory, simple, tender, heavenly." God requires such family worship, the Lord Jesus is worthy of it, Scripture demands it, conscience approves it, and children profit from it. Specific reasons for family worship include:

- The eternal welfare of your spouse, your children, and your own soul

- The satisfaction of a good conscience

- A powerful tool to assist you in rearing children

- The brevity of life

- Love for the glory of God and the welfare of His church

Heed the advice of J. W. Alexander, who wrote: "Fly at once, with your household, to the throne of grace." Beg the Lord to bless your feeble efforts and save your children. Plead with Him to take your covenant children into His arms for all eternity.

Catechizing

The word "catechism" derives from the Greek word *katecheo*, which consists of two words, *kata*, meaning "down toward," and *echeo*, meaning "to sound." *Katacheo* is to "sound down," to speak to someone with the goal of receiving something back as an echo. The catechetical method of questioning sends out the Word and its doctrines to hear responses, to receive back answers that probe the heart and gauge the depth of knowledge.

The New Testament speaks often of catechizing. Luke says that he wrote his gospel "that thou mightest know the certainty of those things, wherein thou hast been instructed [catechized]" (Luke 1:4). Apollos was "catechized" in the way of the Lord (Acts 18). Catechizing obeys the Spirit's command through Paul to Timothy, "These things command and teach" (1 Tim. 4:11).

Parental catechizing is almost a lost art today, to the great loss of families and churches. John J. Murray writes, "We believe it is to the discontinuance of this practice [of catechizing] that we can trace much of the doctrinal ignorance, confusion and instability so characteristic of modern Christianity."[6]

Catechizing sorely needs reviving. "Home-catechization" was the backbone of the Reformed church in its early centuries. The Puritans in particular were great catechists. They believed that pulpit messages should be reinforced by personalized ministry through *catechesis*—the instruction in the doctrines of Scripture using catechisms. Parents were expected to reserve a special time each week, in addition to family worship, in which they catechized their children in the Reformed doctrines of grace.[7]

The Puritans teach us much about home-catechization. Puritan catechizing was evangelistic in several ways:

First, scores of Puritans reached out evangelistically to children and young people by writing catechism books that explained fundamental Christian doctrines via ques-

---

6. "Catechizing — A Forgotten Practice," *Banner of Truth* no. 27 (Oct. 1962):15.

7. Sisemore, 93–94.

tions and answers supported by Scripture.[8] For example, John Cotton titled his catechism, *Milk for Babes, drawn out of the Breasts of both Testaments*.[9] Other Puritans included in the titles of their catechisms such expressions as "the main and fundamental points," "the sum of the Christian religion," the "several heads" or "first principles" of religion, and "the ABC of Christianity." At various levels in the church as well as in the homes of their parishioners, Puritan ministers taught rising generations both from the Bible and from their catechisms. Their goals were to explain the fundamental teachings of the Bible, to help young people commit the Bible to memory, to make sermons and the sacraments more understandable, to prepare covenant children for confession of faith, to teach them how to defend their faith against error, and to help parents teach their own children.[10]

Second, catechizing was evangelistic in relation to both sacraments. When the Westminster Larger Catechism speaks of "improving" (that is, making good use of) one's baptism, it refers to a task of lifelong instruc-

---

8. See George Edward Brown, "Catechists and Catechisms of Early New England" (D.R.E. dissertation, Boston University, 1934); R. M. E. Paterson, "A Study in Catechisms of the Reformation and Post-Reformation Period" (M.A. thesis, Durham University, 1981); P. Hutchinson, "Religious Change: The Case of the English Catechism, 1560–1640" (Ph.D. dissertation, Stanford University, 1984); Ian Green, *The Christian's ABC: Catechisms and Catechizing in England* c. 1530–1740 (Oxford: Clarendon Press, 1996).

9. London, 1646.

10. Cf. W. G. T. Shedd, *Homiletics and Pastoral Theology* (London: Banner of Truth Trust reprint, 1965), 356–75.

tion in which catechisms such as the Shorter Catechism play a decisive role.[11] William Perkins said that the ignorant should memorize his catechism, *The Foundation of Christian Religion*, so they would be "fit to receive the Lord's Supper with comfort." And William Hopkinson wrote in the preface to *A Preparation into the Waie of Life*, that he labored to lead his catechumens "into the right use of the Lord's Supper, a special confirmation of God's promises in Christ."[12]

The more their public efforts to purify the church were crushed, the more the Puritans turned to the home as a bastion for religious instruction and influence. They wrote books on family worship and the "godly order of family government." Robert Openshawe prefaced his catechism with an appeal "to those who were wont to ask how you should spend the long winter evenings, [to] turn to singing of psalms and teaching your household and praying with them."[13]

Finally, catechizing was evangelistic as a way of examining people's spiritual conditions, and for encour-

---

11. The Westminster Assembly desired to establish one catechism and one confession of faith for both England and Scotland, but a spate of catechisms continued to be written after the Westminster standards were drafted (J. Lewis Wilson, "Catechisms, and Their Use Among the Puritans," in *One Steadfast High Intent* [London: Puritan and Reformed Studies Conference, 1966], 41–42).

12. *A Preparation into the Waie of Life, with a Direction into the righte use of the Lordes Supper* (London, 1583), sig. A.3.

13. *Short Questions and Answeares* (London, 1580), A.4.

aging and admonishing them to flee to Christ. Baxter
and his two assistants spent two full days each week
catechizing parishioners in their homes. In addition to
that, on Monday and Tuesday afternoons and evenings
he catechized each of his seven family members for an
hour per week. Those visits involved patiently teaching, gently examining, and carefully leading family and
church members to Christ through the Scriptures. J. I.
Packer concludes: "To upgrade the practice of personal
catechising from a preliminary discipline for children
to a permanent ingredient in evangelism and pastoral
care for all ages was Baxter's main contribution to the
development of Puritan ideals for the ministry."[14]

Puritan churches and schools considered catechism
instruction so important that some even appointed
official catechists. At Cambridge University, William
Perkins served as catechist at Christ's College and John
Preston, at Emanuel College. The Puritan ideal, according to Thomas Gataker, was that a school is a "little
church" and its teachers "private catechists."[15]

Puritan evangelism, carried on by preaching, pastoral admonition, and catechizing, took time and skill.[16]

---

14. *A Quest for Godliness: The Puritan Vision of the Christian
Life* (Wheaton, Ill.: Crossway Books, 1990), 305.

15. *David's Instructor* (London, 1620), 18; see also B. Simon,
"Leicestershire Schools 1635–40," *British Journal of Educational
Studies* (Nov. 1954):47–51.

16. Thomas Boston, *The Art of Manfishing: A Puritan's View
of Evangelism* (Fearn, Ross-shire: Christian Focus reprint,
1998), 14–15.

The Puritans were not looking for quick and easy conversions; they were committed to building up lifelong believers whose hearts, minds, wills, and affections were won to the service of Christ.[17]

The hard work of the Puritan catechist was greatly rewarded. Richard Greenham claimed that catechism teaching built up the Reformed church and did serious damage to Roman Catholicism.[18] When Baxter was installed at Kidderminster in Worcestershire, perhaps one family in each street honored God in family worship; at the end of his ministry there, there were streets where every family did so. He could say that of the six hundred converts that were brought to faith under his preaching, he could not name one that had backslidden to the ways of the world. How vastly different was that result compared to the results of today's evangelists who press for mass conversions, then turn over the hard work of follow-up to others!

Here's some practical advice on how to catechize your children today:

1. Catechize your children at least once a week. Thirty minutes is sufficient for younger children; 45–60 minutes is more appropriate for interested teenagers. If

17. Thomas Hooker, *The Poor Doubting Christian Drawn to Christ* (Worthington, Penn.: Maranatha reprint, 1977).

18. *A Short Forme of Catechising* (London: Richard Bradocke, 1599).

they're not being catechized in church or at school, you should catechize more frequently.

2. Arm yourself with sound Reformed catechism books. For older children, for example, you could use the Heidelberg Catechism, the Westminster Shorter Catechism, or both. You could also use a catechism based on these catechisms, such as that of John Brown or Matthew Henry.[19] Or you could use a program of books. Here's one set of books that covers grades K–12 and has Teachers' Guides for every volume:

K–1   *Bible Questions and Answers* (Carrine Mackenzie)

2–3   *The Truths of God's Word* (Diana Kleyn/ Joel Beeke)

4–5   *Bible Doctrine for Younger Children, Books A and B* (James Beeke)

6–7   *Bible Doctrine for Older Children, Books A and B* (James Beeke)

8–12 *Bible Doctrine for Teens and Young Adults, Books 1, 2, 3* (James Beeke)[20]

---

19. John Brown (of Haddington), *An Essay towards an Easy, Plain, Practical, and Extensive Explication of the Assembly's Shorter Catechism* (New York: Robert Carter, 1849); Matthew Henry, "A Scripture Catechism," in *The Complete Works of Matthew Henry* (Edinburgh: Fullarton & Co., 1855), 2:174–263. See also Henry's prefatory sermon, "The Catechizing of Youth," ibid., 2:157–73.

20. Three series of books cover grades 4–12 that move through the entire scope of Reformed doctrine on increasingly deeper

Another approach would be to teach doctrine from a classic like John Bunyan's *Pilgrim's Progress*.

1. Assign your children questions to memorize, then pack your teaching with questions that flow out of the questions memorized. Draft five to ten questions off of the questions that your catechists are to memorize. Remember, catechizing is not lecturing. Dialogue with your children. Question, re-question, correct, explain, encourage, guide, and review with your catechists.

2. Mix your teaching with numerous illustrations taken from Scripture and daily life. Use poetry, metaphors, similes, acrostics (i.e., every word or line beginning with a particular letter, such as Psalm 119), parallelisms (i.e., two or more lines expressing thoughts in parallel relationships to each other, such as Psalm 119:105), and various mnemonics (i.e., techniques of improving the memory, such as "TULIP" for the Five Points of Calvinism) to make doctrine stick and come alive. Use your catechism as a map to guide your children through the Scriptures.

3. Prepare each lesson well. Read, study, and memorize. If possible, spend a few hours on each lesson. The souls of your children, and your own spiritual well-being, may well make these hours the most profitable of your week.

---

levels. All of these books are available from Reformation Heritage Books. For an excellent bibliography of Selected Confessions and Catechisms, see Donald VanDyken, *Rediscovering Catechism: The Art of Equipping Covenant Children* (Phillipsburg, N.J.: P & R, 2000), 115–31.

4. Begin each catechism lesson with Psalm-singing, Scripture reading, prayer, and review of the last lesson. Ask one of your children to close with prayer.

5. Persevere in love. Even when you don't see fruits, press on in prayer, preparation, and teaching. Teach winsomely, with passion and love. Children are rarely fooled; we need to show love for the Word and the doctrines we teach. Keep reaching for greater depth. The gospel's simplicity is precious but that simplicity never robs it of profundity. Aim to raise stalwart, doctrinally knowledgeable sons and daughters who will, by grace, hold fast the Reformed faith with conviction. In dependency on the Spirit, aim to bring your children, who are the heritage of the Lord, to the Lord who is the heritage of covenant children. Pray that your children, by grace, will love instruction and the God of the truths taught.

May God help us today to view the evangelizing of our covenant children as a task that involves both bringing the gospel to them and so presenting Christ and the doctrines of grace that believing children may grow in Him. We need to recover the vision of our forebears in our catechizing, such that we view evangelism as entailing both how to come to Christ and how to live out of Christ.[21]

---

21. For books on teaching catechism, see Joyce M. Horton, *How to Teach the Catechism to Children* (Jackson, Miss.: Reformed Theological Seminary, 1979); Starr Meade, *Training Hearts, Teaching Minds: Family Devotions Based on the Shorter Catechism* (Phillipsburg, N.J.: P & R, 2000); VanDyken,

Godly Conversation

Scripture teaches that we must take time each day to speak to our covenant children about God. Serious, spiritual conversation should be done in regular times of family worship and teaching, but also spontaneously through the process of everyday life. As Deuteronomy 6:7 says, "Thou shalt teach them diligently unto thy children, and shalt talk of them when thou sittest in thine house, and when thou walkest by the way, and when thou liest down, and when thou risest up."

Each day includes four basic teaching times:

1. *Rising up.* How we begin our days is so important. With your children, focus on God at the beginning of each day. Scripture and prayer, together with some edifying comments, is a far better way to begin a day than simply grabbing a bowl of cereal and passing your children as they rush to school or play. Spend a few minutes together as a family in communion with the Lord each morning.

2. *Sitting at home.* Many families do not spend enough time at home. Consider reserving at least one evening per week to help keep the family close to God and each other. Talk, eat, read, and spend time together. Pray and speak to one another about God and His Word. Family nights are wonderful times for spiritual conversation, teaching, and edification.

Rediscovering Catechism: The Art of Equipping Covenant Children. VanDyken includes an excellent annotated bibliography.

3. *Walking by the way.* When we walk with our children or ride somewhere with them in the car, we have wonderful opportunites to instruct them about God and the way to live. Our reactions to the events and challenges of our daily lives is also a powerful teaching tool for our children. Show your children as you walk along the road of life how God works and how to make choices that please Him.

4. *Lying down.* Bedtime is a special time to talk with your children. Do you have a nightly routine for instructing them about God? Reading Bible stories or good books, praying, and playing quiet, sacred music are good tools for bringing your children's day to a close. If your children are young, sit next to them on their beds, and speak to them about their day. Assure them of your love. Invite them to share their failures, challenges, and prayer concerns. One way to do this is to begin by sharing your own.

End the day on a positive note; remove any malice that exists. Help your children count their blessings. Show them how to thank God for the merciful events of the day. Remind them that we need to beseech God to forgive our many sins and to meet our soul's needs at the close of each day. In short, every day of our lives must be punctuated with the truths of God and His grace.

All conversation with your children need not be spiritual. Parents who have a meaningful relationship with their children can talk about the natural and the spiritual and back to the natural again with no discomfort or awkwardness. Learn to draw your child out, and encourage him to discuss anything with you. Don't feel you must have all the answers to everything, but do use sound Reformed commentaries and literature to assist you.[22] Search for answers together with them, or, better yet, train your children how to find some of the answers on their own. Teach them how to use Strong's concordance, various word helps, and commentaries as they grow older.

Learn how to enter your child's life. Enjoy relating to your child where he or she is at. That will mean different things at different ages, such as wrestling with your son, walking in the woods, drawing him out in talking about his friends, striving to understand his feelings, and discussing his goals and dreams. If that relating is not done successfully, we will not hit the target.

In talking with your child, you'll be taking the spiritual temperature of that child. So get to the heart of the matter. Discern what your child is capable of understanding, then, adjusting your vocabulary accordingly, tell the child what is involved in becoming a Christian. Don't wait until the child raises the subject; you must initiate it.

The Hebrew word for instruction in Deuteronomy 6:7 says that we are to "sharpen" or "impress" upon our children the teachings of God's Word. The idea is that we are to mark, brand, penetrate, and disciple our chil-

---

22. For an introductory guide, see Joel R. Beeke, *A Reader's Guide to Reformed Literature: An Annotated Bibliography of Reformed Theology* (Grand Rapids: Reformation Heritage Books, 1999).

dren in God's ways. That is our daily calling. Remember, it takes time and diligence to make a lasting impression (Isa. 28:9–10). As fossils contain deep impressions, so we are to leave impressions of God's truth upon our children that will last for a lifetime and beyond.

Godly Models

If we would have godly children, they must see God's character in our lives. Though they may learn much from what we say and do, they will learn most from who we are. Our praying, teaching, and living must be one; we must be and practice what we pray. "God cannot resist a parent's prayer when it is sufficiently backed up with a parent's sanctification," wrote Alexander Whyte.[23]

We must not fail to act as our children's spiritual mentors. Besides the Bible, our lives are the most important book our children will ever read. What do they read in the pages of our lives?

We can be no better as parents than we are as persons. Our lives must display love for God, our neighbors, and our children as well as proper love for the value of our own souls. We must strive for balance in all our relations. God instructs us in the verses prior to Deuteronomy 6:7 that we are to love God with all our heart, soul, and might. Love for God must motivate us to love our children unconditionally—but not their sins. We must model the gracious unfailing love of the Tri-

---

23. *Lord, Teach Us To Pray* (Grand Rapids: Baker reprint, 1976), 124.

une God for His children even as He hates their sins. Such unconditional love is a special calling and opportunity given to us, for love for their persons may touch the hearts of our children and make them tender in ways that all our admonition can never accomplish.

How will our children see this love in us towards God, themselves, and others? Mostly through our words and actions as we move through the day. In this, they will see and instinctively feel:

- How important God, prayer, the Bible, and worship are to us, and whether we approach God with eager expectation or out of a mere sense of duty.

- How much time and energy we spend in spiritual devotion.

- How we respond to affliction.

- If we really believe that all things work together for good for those that love God (Rom. 8:28), that not a hair can fall from our head without the Father's will.

- If we are repenting parents who hate sin, trust in Jesus Christ, and joy in the Holy Spirit .

- If we grieve mostly over selfish things or over things that grieve God.

- If our marriage reflects the Bridegroom-bride/Christ-church models of Ephesians 5.

- If we enjoy praying, talking, playing, vacationing, and being with our children.

- If we're willing to deny ourselves for our children's sake.

- If we discipline our children appropriately and with love, or inappropriately and in anger.

- How we approach our vocation—as a calling from God in which we strive to use our talents for His glory, or as a selfish endeavor in which we imbibe the world's mentality of working for the weekend.

- How we treat those who offend us, spread rumors about us, or are our enemies.

- If we are kind, compassionate, and forgiving to others (Eph. 4:32), and spur them on to love and good deeds (Heb. 10:24).

- If we pray for others (James 5:16) and offer them hospitality without grumbling (1 Peter 4:9).

- If we rejoice with those that rejoice and mourn with those that mourn (Rom. 12:15).

- How we honor those in authority over us, such as policemen, the government, and office-bearers.

As our children grow older, they become more astute at measuring our lives against the Beatitudes or the fruits of the Spirit. They will test Christianity in us, asking such questions as, Is the Christian life worth living? How we act as parents will be the most influential answers to this question.

Children need to see the gospel authenticated by us. We are the living gospel (cf. 2 Cor. 3:1–3), for better or worse. Our children's idea of God will be shaped by what we teach and who we are. If we do what God requires, we will be able to say to our children when they become adults and move out of our homes, "Continue thou in the things which thou hast learned and hast been assured of, knowing of whom thou hast learned them; and that from a child thou hast known the holy scriptures, which are able to make thee wise unto salvation through faith which is in Christ Jesus" (2 Tim. 3:14–15).

Consider, too, involving other believers in the lives of your children, such as elderly saints, "mothers in Israel," God-fearing grandparents, missionaries, and Christian pen pals. The covenant community is rich in such persons and, with the Spirit's blessing, they can be a great help to you and your children in modeling and mentoring living Christianity.

Finally, use special occasions in the church to assist you in modeling Christianity. For example, the funeral services of the congregation present an important occasion rich in opportunities to evangelize children. A pre-schooler can feel the reality of death beside an open coffin and may ask significant questions. Children should not be strangers to the house of mourning, or even to the face of death. Older children can also be profitably engaged in ministry to the sick, the grieving, and the aged members of the church. Model such involvement for your children, and draw them into serving others commensurate with their age and opportunities.

How can we live up to such a calling? We must begin by repenting of our indwelling sin, our inconsistent walk, our ignorance of the Bible, and our failure to evangelize our children. Then we must, with holy fear and solemn conviction, realize our covenantal responsibilities to our children and take refuge in God, treasuring the covenantal promises and grace He desires to bestow for Christ's sake upon unworthy parents. As Robert L. Dabney says:

> The instrumentalities of the family are chosen and ordained of God as the most efficient of all means of grace—more truly and efficaciously means of saving grace than all the other ordinances of the church. To family piety are given the best promises of the gospel, under the new, as well as under the old dispensation. How, then, should a wise God do otherwise than consecrate the Christian family, and ordain that the believing parents shall sanctify the children? Hence, the very foundation of all parental fidelity to children's souls is to be laid in the conscientious, solemn, and hearty adoption of the very duties and promises which God seals in the covenant of infant baptism.[24]

24. *Discussions: Evangelical and Theological* (London: Banner of Truth Trust reprint, 1967), 1:693.

Concluding Applications |4|

Psalm 103:17–18 says, "The mercy of the Lord is from everlasting to everlasting upon them that fear him, and his righteousness unto children's children; to such as keep his covenant, and to those that remember his commandments to do them." This text sets forth a three-step program that summarizes Christian parenting: first, to keep watch over and prepare one's own heart ("fear the Lord"); second, to be faithful in all the duties of the covenant ("keep His covenant"); and third, to live according to God's commandments before one's children and to act towards them as God commands ("remember His commandments to do them"), which includes instruction, nurture, and admonition.

Leading a child to Christ involves much more than the few minutes it takes to lead him or her in the "sinner's prayer." It is not a one-time event. Some thoughts you should keep in mind:

1. *Leading a child to Christ is a journey—usually a long journey—in which you must be radically dependent upon the Spirit of Christ*. You cannot effect your chil-

dren's conversion; only the Holy Spirit can do that. Our hope is that the sovereign Holy Spirit delights to convert covenant children as much as the Father delights in saving them from generation to generation and the Son delights in suffering them to come unto Him.

The triune God's sovereign, electing grace is always the primary cause of our children's conversion, which God is pleased to work out through the secondary causes of the means of grace. The same Holy Spirit, who convicts us of our sin and leads us to Christ and into the pathways of holiness, is also faithful to comfort us, teach us, and lead us in evangelizing our children, making it fruitful.

Depending on the Holy Spirit will help us become more sensitive to the spiritual needs of our children and our impossibilities. He will provide us with greater wisdom and patience than if we try to convert our children in our own strength.[1]

2. *Evangelize your children at every opportunity, for the window of opportunity is rapidly closing.* Parenting is like archery. When our children are young, we have the privilege of getting shots up close. In later years, the target is at a greater distance. As parents, we must take advantage of the times when our children are young, for when they become older, they may go off to college, move away, or get married.

---

1. J. Oswald Sanders, *Effective Evangelism* (Fearn, Ross-shire: Christian Focus reprint, 1999), 116–18.

As parental marksmen, we only get a few shots per target. Once our children have been released into the world, they are on their own. We cannot stop them from going there, though we can still pray for them. Cherish each arrow, each opportunity, in your quiver. Sharpen those arrows and pray that you may be the archer for Christ that your children need. Pray that the Holy Spirit may direct your arrows to lead your children to find the one Mediator between God and man, Christ Jesus.

3. *Don't abandon your post as marksman until you see fruits in your children such as conviction of sin, righteousness, and judgment; regeneration and conversion; repentance and faith; sanctification and perseverance.* Don't rest until you see in them signs of spiritual poverty, mourning over sin, meekness before God, hungering and thirsting after Christ's righteousness, mercifulness, pureness of heart, and joyous cross-bearing under persecution (Matt. 5:3–12). Press on until you see fruits of the Spirit: "love, joy, peace, longsuffering, gentleness, goodness, faith, meekness, temperance" (Gal. 5:22–23).[2]

Richard Mather once preached a sermon that included what covenant children on the way to hell might say to their negligent parents. On the Day of

---

2. For fruits of grace found in a converted child, see Archibald Alexander, *Thoughts on Religious Experience* (Edinburgh: Banner of Truth Trust reprint, 1967), 11–20; Wilhelmus à Brakel, *The Christian's Reasonable Service*, trans. Bartel Elshout, ed. Joel R. Beeke (Grand Rapids: Reformation Heritage Books, 2003), 2:249.

Judgment they would say, "All this that we here suffer is through you. You should have taught us the things of God and did not. You should have restrained us from sin and corrected us, and you did not. You were the means of our original corruption and guiltiness, and yet you never showed any competent care that we might be delivered from it. Woe unto us that we had such carnal and careless parents. And woe unto you that you had no more compassion and pity to prevent the everlasting misery of your own children."[3]

God forbid that our children would ever say such things to us. Rather, let us pray that we can say when they leave home as young adults: "My dear son (or daughter), you know that we have taught you God's Word and wrestled for your soul. Though we were far from perfect, we have set a God-fearing example before you. You didn't see in us a sinless piety but you did see an unfeigned faith. You know we sought first the kingdom of God and His righteousness. Your conscience will bear witness to the fact that Christ was the center of this home. We sang together, prayed together, and talked about the truths and ways of God. If you turn away from all this light and these privileges and insist on going your own way, we can only pray the more that all our Bible study, praying, and singing will not rise up against you in the day of judgment. See to it, by God's grace, that we will not have to stand on the

---

3. Quoted by Jim Elliff, "How Children Come to Faith in Christ" (radio address).

Day of Judgment on the right side of Christ and see you standing on His left side."

"Happy indeed," wrote J. C. Ryle, "is the father who can say with Robert Bolton on his deathbed to his children: 'I do believe that not one of you will dare to meet me at the tribunal of Christ in an unregenerate state.'"

4. *Finally, remember it is never too late to begin evangelizing your children.* Some of you may say, "This message is too late for me. What if I have failed all my life to evangelize my children?"

It is not too late. Your sin has been serious, but you may still do the following:

- Pray for your children. God can make crooked sticks straight, even after your departure. Years after Hezekiah died, God answered his prayers and converted Manasseh (2 Chr. 33:9–13).

- Confess your sin to them, asking their forgivness for not evangelizing them.

- Speak to your grandchildren, and bring them the gospel.

- Speak to the children of the church to which you belong.

- Consider the possibility of assisting in your church's Sunday school and other ministries to children.

- Engage in serious family worship with your spouse, beginning where you should have begun decades ago.[4]

---

4. Edward N. Gross, *Will My Children Go To Heaven? Hope*

Children bring us great joy and great anxiety. They delight us and frustrate us. Loving them means leading them in the ways of God, for their greatest pleasure will be found in knowing and serving Him. May God help us all to lead children and grandchildren in the ways of God, for "of such is the kingdom of God."

We close with the prayer of a seventeenth-century Puritan:

> O God, I cannot endure to see the destruction of my kindred. Let those that are united to me in tender ties be precious in thy sight and devoted to thy glory. Sanctify and prosper my domestic devotion, instruction, discipline, example, that my house may be a nursery for heaven, my church the garden of the Lord, enriched with the trees of righteousness of thy planting, for thy glory. Let not those of my family who are amiable, moral, attractive, fall short of heaven at last. Grant that the promising appearances of tender conscience, soft heart, the alarms and delights of thy Word, be not finally blotted out, but bring forth judgment unto victory in all whom I love.[5]

---

and Help for Believing Parents (Phillipsburg, N.J.: P & R, 1995), see chapter 12, "Encouragement for Parents Who Fail."

5. Arthur Bennett, ed., *The Valley of Vision* (Edinburgh: Banner of Truth Trust, 1975), 113.

A Loving Encouragement to Flee Worldliness

And open letter written to parents to encourage them and their children to flee worldliness.

Dear parents,

God has greatly blessed you with a child whom you would have baptized. Baptism involves many privileges and many responsibilities. One of those responsibilities is that you strive to the utmost of your power to keep yourselves and your covenant children from worldliness. Baptism obliges us to "forsake the world" (Form for the Administration of Baptism).

In our day, love of the world wars against biblical, covenantal child-rearing. God's Word encourages us to flee worldliness. First John 2:15–17 says, "Love not the world, neither the things that are in the world. If any man love the world, the love of the Father is not in him. For all that is in the world, the lust of the flesh, and the lust of the eyes, and the pride of life, is not of the Father, but is of the world. And the world passeth away, and the lust thereof: but he that doeth the will of God abideth for ever."

The Essence of Worldliness

In this passage, the apostle John contrasts love for the world with love for the Father. These two loves are incompatible. Either you love God or you love the world; you cannot love both. As Jesus said, "No man can serve two masters: for either he will hate the one, and love the other; or else he will hold to the one, and despise the other" (Matt. 6:24).

One love must rule our life: one holy passion for God and the things of God. The choice is clear and the directions simple, but the way is not easy. The appeal of the world is strong, and the flesh is weak. As Jesus said, "Watch and pray, that ye enter not into temptation: the spirit indeed is willing, but the flesh is weak" (Matt. 26:41).

John offers two important reasons why we should not love the world or the things of the world. First, the world is opposed to God. To follow John's reasoning, we must understand his use of the Greek word *kosmos*, or "world," which has several meanings in the New Testament. In 1 John 2:15–17, the apostle is not referring to the physical world in which we live nor the mass of people living on the planet. Rather, he uses the term to refer to a kingdom, its ruler and its inhabitants, lost in sin and wholly at odds with anything divine or pleasing to God. He is talking about Satan's kingdom of darkness that includes all people who are under his dominion and live according to the standards of this world. John Calvin used the word in this sense to include "everything connected with the present life, apart from the kingdom of God and the hope of eternal life."

In our text, John uses the word to mean a realm that is antithetical to God. "World" here has an ethical, spiritual connotation, set in contrast with Christ and His church. This world does not know God or His Son but crucified the Lord of glory (John 1:10). It refers to "this present evil world" (John 8:23) as opposed to the other world, the heavenly world.

This world, though created to reflect the glory of God, now lives in rebellion against the Lord and against His Christ (Ps. 2:2). It has become a fallen, disordered world lying in the grip of the evil one, says 1 John 5:19. This world, despite its great achievements, is lost. It is incapable of saving itself. It has lost its meaning. It can no longer glorify God. In this sense, the world is the mass of mankind who are estranged from God through sin and lives after the lusts of the flesh. It is populated by sinful men, women, and children who focus on this world and neglect the world to come.

Worldly people think more of their bodies than their souls, more about pleasing men than pleasing God. Their motto is to move forward rather than upward. Their goal is outward prosperity rather than holiness. They worship the creature rather than the Creator. They lack reverence. They burst with selfish desires rather than heartfelt supplications. They may not deny God, but they do ignore and forget Him.

Worldliness, then, is human activity without God. Someone who is of this world is controlled by what preoccupies the world: the quest for pleasure, profit, and position. He yields to the spirit of fallen mankind: the spirit of self-seeking, self-indulgence without regard for God. Each one of us, by nature, was born as a worldling. We are attached to the world. We are in tune with the spirit of the world. We belong to this evil world; it is our natural habitat.

By nature we also possess a carnal mind that is at enmity with God and is "not subject to the law of God, neither indeed can be" (Rom. 8:7). As much as we were nourished via an umbilical cord in our mother's womb, so we were born with an umbilical cord that ties us to the world. Consequently, our understanding is darkened (Eph. 4:18) as we enter the world. The guilt of Adam's sin is on us, and we inherit the pollution of his sin.

We are dead in our sins and trespasses and are children of wrath (Eph. 2:1–2), until God graciously regenerates us and makes us His own (John 3:5). Only then are we set apart from fallen mankind and called out of this sinful world to become living members of the church and kingdom of God. Regeneration, or the new birth, divides the world into the kingdom of God and the kingdom of Satan. Those kingdoms live at war with each other.

The Christian is still attracted to the world because of the sin that remains in him. The Bible calls this the flesh. Thus, while you must keep yourselves "unspotted from the world," as James says, you must remember that the sinful flesh in us is inclined toward the world. That is why isolation from the world cannot keep us from sin. We who are believers carry a piece of the world within us.

With the world, the devil, and the flesh against you, is there any hope for victory? Absolutely, for that victory was won when Jesus defeated Satan on the cross and rose from the dead. In John 15:19, Jesus said, "Ye are not of the world, but I have chosen you out of the world." Because of His victorious death, God's people have been plucked from the kingdom of this world and now belong to Christ and the kingdom of heaven. Through Jesus Christ, they have overcome the world, the flesh, and the devil. As 1 John 2:13 says, "I write unto you, young men, because ye have overcome the wicked one."

In 1 John 5:4 we read, "For whatsoever is born of God overcometh the world: and this is the victory that overcometh the world, even our faith." In Christ, by the Spirit's grace, we have overcome the world, but we must also fight daily against the temptations of the world. John names three ways in which we are lured into the ways of the world: the lust of the flesh, the lust of the eyes, and the pride of life.

The Paths of Worldliness

Verse 16 specifically tells us, "For all that is in the world, the lust of the flesh, and the lust of the eyes, and the pride of life, is not of the Father, but is of the world." We must likewise be specific as we warn one another about separating ourselves and our children from those paths of worldliness named by John.

First, we must beware of "the lust of the flesh." We must not love a world that delights in the lusts of the flesh. That means resisting many temptations, such as substance abuse, whether in the form of drugs, smoking, overeating, or excessive drinking of alcohol. The Bible repeatedly warns against gluttony and drunkenness. We must not be brought under bondage to anything physical but are to be self-controlled, for our body is the temple of the Holy Ghost (1 Cor. 6:12; 9:27; 3:17). We must show our children that we treat it as such.

The prohibition against fleshly lusting forbids sexual immorality in all its forms. It forbids any flirtation or physical intimacy outside of marriage. God has wisely placed sexual intimacy within the secure bond of marriage. We must let our children enjoy the security of a solid, loving relationship between their father and mother.

We must also be modest about the way we dress, so that it does not encourage lust. Clothing that accents our nakedness arouses fleshly lusts that offend God, who blames those who provoke lust as much as those who lust after them. Here, too, we must be an example for our children as we lovingly, yet firmly, require them to walk and dress modestly.

Refusing to love the world means keeping ourselves and our children from worldly parties, unedifying entertainment, night clubs, and dancing, all of which excite the lusts of the flesh. It also includes turning away from all worldly music that either in its lyrics or its beat promotes the lusts of the flesh. Of all the music that we and our children listen to, we must ask: Can I pray over this music? Does it glorify God or ignite fleshly lusts? Does it pass the test of Philippians 4:8, being "honest, just, pure, lovely, and of good report"? If it encourages lust, rid yourself of it.

Do not love this present evil world, for your own sake and the sake of your baptized children. Rather, "Put ye on the Lord Jesus Christ, and make not provision for the flesh, to fulfil the lusts thereof" (Rom. 13:14).

Second, John warns against the "lust of the eyes." How active Satan is in engaging our eyes, tempting us to indulge in worldly entertainment. Just as he tempted our first parents to believe that their Creator was a hard, legalistic God, so he whispers to us, "Has God said that you cannot partake of any of today's entertainment? Has He told you that you may not watch movies that tempt your eyes? Does He want you to live a boring life, like David, who said in Psalm 101 that he would set no wicked thing before his eyes? If so, isn't He a hard, legalistic God?"

Satan has been using such arguments for thousands of years. He still acts the part of the wily serpent, seeking to entice and seduce you and your children. He knows his time is short, so he will do anything to persuade people to look at the evil fruit hanging from the tree of worldly entertainment, which looks so pleasant and promises to make us wise in the ways of this world. Perhaps he'll even use a friend to entice you, as he used Eve to tempt Adam. Satan is a master at hiding himself under the cloak of friendship.

Today Satan makes such fruit even more tempting by persuading parents to bring it into the home. He provides videos that are as bad or worse than those at the theater or on the Internet, so that you can watch them in the privacy of your own home.

Dear parents, love not the world. Say no to all forms of video and Internet entertainment that pander to the lust of the eyes by glamorizing sin. Such forms of entertainment make adultery and fornication look innocent, commonplace, or else exciting. Murder becomes thrilling. Profanity is acceptable everyday speech. We cannot trust our own strength in this, for we can persuade ourselves that something good can be gleaned from such entertainment. None of us have acquired the spiritual maturity of the apostle Paul, yet even he had to admit, "For I know that in me (that is, in my flesh,) dwelleth no good thing: for to will is present with me; but how to perform that which is good I find not. For the good that I would I do not: but the evil which I would not, that I do" (Rom. 7:18–19).

The same principle applies to television. The vast majority of the shows on television are anti-Christian. They are harmful to our spiritual life and growth. Like Job, let us make a covenant with our eyes that we will set no wicked thing before us (Job 31:1). Please consider, for the welfare of your own souls as well as those of your children, not to bring television into your homes. We are convinced that most television-viewing is harmful to our spiritual well-being.

Let us rid our homes also of unedifying magazines, trashy love novels, and profane books; indeed, all printed and visual material that contradicts the Ten Commandments. How can we pray not to be led into temptation while we continue to play with the fire of temptation? As James warns us, "Every man is tempted, when he is drawn away of his own lust, and enticed. Then when lust hath conceived, it bringeth forth sin: and sin, when it is finished, bringeth forth death" (James 1:14–15).

Flee the lusts of the eyes. Practice self-denial. Follow Paul, who said, "Herein do I exercise myself, to have always a conscience void of offense toward God, and toward men" (Acts 24:16).

Finally, John warns against "the pride of life." How prevalent such pride is in our hearts. As George Swinnock said, "Pride is the first shirt we put on in Paradise and the last we will take off when we die." The pride of life includes:

1. Pride in ourselves and our accomplishments. Such pride is at the root of our hearts. By nature we are filled with self-gratification, self-contentment, and self-fulfilment. We want to rule our own destiny. We live for ourselves, applauding our own wisdom and accomplishments.

2. Pride of false religions. Religions in the world that challenge Scripture by teaching that man must do something to find favor with God are false religions. They include free-will Christianity, which claims that

fallen man can do anything to contribute to his salvation. Such religion oozes with pride.

3. Pride in challenging the governing providence of
God. This includes traditional sects such as Mormon-
ism and Jehovah's Witnesses, as well as Free Masonry
and other secret lodges. It refers to all practices of the
New Age Movement, transcendental meditation, and
the occult, such as fortune-telling, horoscopes, ouija
boards, and palm-reading. If refers to attempts to
destroy life through artificial birth control, abortion, or
euthanasia, all of which try to usurp the power of divine
providence.

4. Pride of idolizing movie actors, sports heroes, government leaders, or other popular figures. John condemns
all human idolization as the pride of life.

5. Pride of materialism. The love of money is the heart
of the pride of life. Loving possessions such as our
homes or cars or clothing more than God is idolatrous;
it feeds our quest for pleasure and gratification with
status symbols. Dishonesty in business, tax evasion,
and other unethical ways of increasing personal wealth
feed the pride of life. So do covetousness or inordinate
desires to become rich at the expense of our own and
our family's spiritual welfare. Pride of life involves
gambling, lotteries, and everything that is contrary to
good stewardship in which our firstfruits must be given
to the Lord.

6. Pride of desecrating the Lord's Day and neglecting worship services. How proud we must be to think that we don't need to set one day aside to worship the Lord and to receive the kind of spiritual food that will nurture us for the coming week. Let us set the pattern of Sabbath worship for ourselves as well as for our dear children.

Dear friends, I trust that enough has been said to show the sins of the deadly paths that lead to worldliness: the lust of the flesh, the lust of the eyes, and the pride of life. We pray that you may set a God-fearing example to help your covenant children avoid these paths. Ask yourselves as parents: Which path are we most prone to walk down? Do we engage in holy warfare against all three of these paths? Do we walk different from the world? Are we pilgrims and strangers on the earth? My people "shall dwell alone, and shall not be reckoned among the nations," God says in Numbers 23:9. Can that be said of us? Do we love the Father, or do we love the world? Eternal consequences hinge upon our answers to these questions.

The Curse of Worldliness

God curses worldliness, John says, for "the world passeth away, and the lust thereof" (v. 17). That's the second reason John cites for not loving the world. The world's best pleasures are temporary. The world is our passage, not our portion. Our death dates are on God's calendar. As Hebrews 9:27 says, "It is appointed unto men once to die, but after this the judgment."

The world will one day be burned up, together with all of those who lust. So if you fill your life with the lust of the flesh, the lust of the eye, and the pride of life, what have you acquired? A worldly life that contradicts the vows you undertake at baptism, destroys your family and ultimately ends in damnation. All the lusts for which people sold their souls, ruined their families, and stained their reputations—what is left when these lusts have passed away? Nothing but a gnawing worm that will never die and the wrath of God. Despite your hard work, your daily anxiety, and your pursuit of pleasure, that is all that the love of the world can do for you. As Spurgeon said, "If you had got all the world, you would have got nothing after your coffin lid was screwed down but gravedust in your mouth."

Dear parents, let us realize that the world is temporary, vain, and unworthy of your attention. The world never gives what it promises. It is a gigantic mirage, a tragic fraud, a hollow bubble. As John Trapp wrote, "Pleasure, profit, and preferment are the worldling's trinity." Long ago, Solomon discovered all three to be vanity. When you read Ecclesiastes, you will understand why John Bunyan called the world Vanity Fair. You also will realize why James asked: "Know ye not that the friendship of the world is enmity with God? Whosoever will be a friend of the world is the enemy of God" (4:4).

Deliverance from Worldliness

God delivers His people from worldliness in three ways:

1. *Initial deliverance.* Every true work of grace in the heart of a sinner includes radical deliverance from the world and a lifestyle of worldliness. The umbilical cord that tied us to the womb of worldliness is cut when we are born into the kingdom of God. This happens for two reasons. First, Christ died to cut the cord between sinners and the world. As Galatians 1:4 says, Christ "gave himself for our sins, that he might deliver us from this present evil world, according to the will of God and our Father." Christ didn't come just to deliver His people from eternal condemnation, great as that is, but it was the Father's will that Christ would also deliver them from this present evil world. All the beatings and spittings that He bore, the shame of His nakedness, the shrouded heavens, and His cry of dereliction happened because He gave Himself for those whom He determined would be wrenched out of this present evil world and brought into the kingdom of God.

Second, the Holy Spirit makes the Father and Son's intention effective in applying the saving virtue of the death of Christ. As Paul says in Galatians 6:14, "God forbid that I should glory, save in the cross of our Lord Jesus Christ, by whom the world is crucified unto me, and I unto the world." The apostle is saying that, by the applying work of the Spirit, the cross of Jesus Christ was so powerful that it made the world totally undesirable to him. The world lost its fair colors and became positively homely.

Dear parents, has the beauty of Christ dimmed the beauty of worldliness for you? Has Christ crucified the power of the world over you? Has the love of the Father in Christ so conquered your love of the world that it no longer has dominion over you?

2. *Continued deliverance.* God works out continued deliverance in the believer's life. In the initial implanting of grace, He breaks the dominion of sin and the world. They no longer reign; however, they do remain in the soul. The remnants of worldliness yet cling to the born-again believer. The desire for the approval of those who are living by the standards and goals of the world is not altogether dead. Believers are still tempted to conform to the world, whether because of peer pressure or the desire for economic advancement.

Deliverance from this kind of inherent worldliness is possible only by doing the will of God, John tells us (v. 17c). But what does that involve?

- We must realize that it is crucial to fight against worldliness. If we are not convinced of that as parents, we will make little progress with ourselves and our children. James 1:27 tells us, "Pure religion and undefiled before God and the Father is this, To visit the fatherless and widows in their affliction, and to keep himself unspotted from the world." The purity of our walk with God is directly related to our commitment that we will not allow any of the world to stain the garments of righteousness that God has given us.

- We must use every means to conquer worldliness. We must listen repeatedly to sermons, saturate ourselves with Scripture, meditate on the Word, read books that can make us wise to salvation, and pray without ceasing. We must fellowship with believers, observe the Lord's Day, evangelize unbelievers, and serve others. We must be good stewards of our time and money. With the Spirit's blessing, our example will be a powerful influence upon our children.

- We must trust our great High Priest and His Spirit. When the power of the world threatens to invade our souls, we can take comfort in remembering that our great High Priest prayed, "Father, I pray not that thou shouldest take them out of the world [here world is used in the sense of this earth], but that thou shouldest keep them from the evil" (John 17:15). When every defense seems down, and we are most vulnerable to yielding to the enemy of our souls, we may yet hope for deliverance through the intercession of Jesus Christ and the preserving power of His Spirit. We may cry out, "Dear Savior, were it not for Thy intercession, and blessed Spirit, for Thy preservation, in the hour of temptation we would have been swept into evil."

As Spurgeon wrote, "I thank God that when temptation is present, He removes my desire, and when desire to sin is present, He removes the temptation."

That, friends, is the gracious gift of Jesus Christ who promises that He will pray for us in the hour of temptation that our faith will not fail (Luke 22:32).

3. *Perfected deliverance.* If we are believers, full deliverance will be ours in the age to come, which, says John, "abideth for ever!" Heaven is in our hearts and in our deepest affections, yet the world and the devil are still at our elbow. But in the age to come, nothing but righteousness will dwell in the new heavens and the new earth. The world that is under the curse of God, and the prince of the power of the air will be no more. Satan and all of his followers will be banished to eternal perdition. And the people of God will shine in the firmament of God's glory.

In conclusion, we all face the danger of worldliness that Paul lamented in Demas who "hath forsaken me, having loved this present world" (2 Tim. 4:10). Though Demas had prayed and worked with Paul, witnessing his tears as he wrote his pastoral letters, Demas eventually forsook the godly apostle because he was bewitched by the world. Dear parents, beware of anything that is rooted in worldly success. We must die to this.

As you strive to fulfil the vows you make when your children are baptized, may Jesus Christ Himself draw near to you with His Word. May God so work in you and your children that the world will lie as dead at your feet as you are dead to the world. May God richly bless you and your children with His covenantal mercies and place His divine approval on all your efforts to preserve your covenant children from the sinful enticements of the world.

Training of Children

O God of Abra'm, hear
The parents' humble cry;
In covenant mercy now appear,
While in the dust we lie.

These children of our love
In mercy Thou hast given,
That we through grace may faithful prove
In training them for heaven.

Oh! grant Thy Spirit, Lord,
Their hearts to sanctify;
Remember now Thy gracious word,
Our hopes on Thee rely.

Draw forth the melting tear,
The penitential sigh;
Inspire their hearts with faith sincere,
And fix their hopes on high.

These children now are Thine,
We give them back to Thee;
Oh! lead them by Thy grace divine,
Along the heavenly way.

—Thomas Hastings

Teaching Children

Lord, assist us by Thy grace,
To instruct our infant race;
Grant us wisdom from above,
Fill us with a Savior's love.

Let us in Thy peace abide,
In Thy promises confide,
While our seed with ready zeal,
Learn of us to do Thy will.

May we teach them day by day,
In the house and by the way,
When they rise or go to rest,
Till Thy truth shall make them blessed.

While in childhood's tender age,
They unfold the sacred page,
May they see in every line,
Kindling rays of light divine.

Precious Savior, hear our prayer,
We commit them to Thy care;
Be their Shepherd and their Guide,
Bring them to Thy bleeding side.

— Anonymous

Scripture Index